The centenary of "A Shropshire lad" : the life & writings of A.E. Houseman - Primary Source Edition

Naiditch, P. G, University of California, Los Angeles. Library. Department of Special Collections

The Centenary of
"A Shropshire Lad"

The Life &
Writings of
A.E. Housman

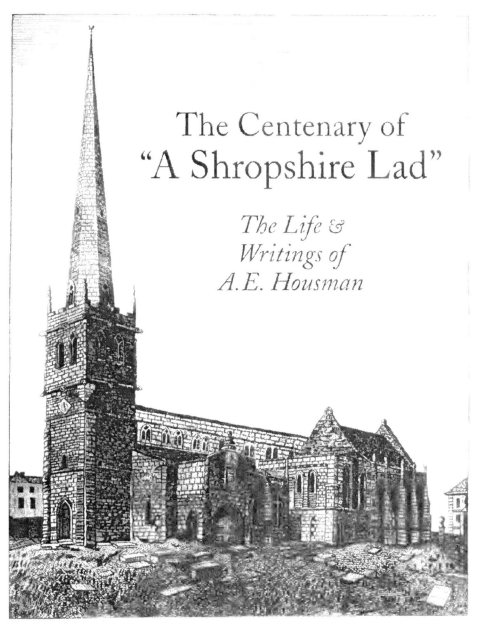

Department of Special Collections
University Research Library
University of California
Los Angeles, 1996

The Centenary of "A Shropshire Lad" the Life and Writings of A E Housman
An Exhibition in the University Research Library January 2 – March 31 1996

Catalogue P G Naiditch

Titlepage design Ellen Watanabe

Illustration J Phillips, *The History and Antiquities of Shrewsbury* London Printed & Sold by T Wood 1779, facing p 90 (St Mary's Church) (UCLA Special Collections DA 690 S58 P5)

The Author is pleased to acknowledge the help of the late Seymour Adelman, Phillip Bevis Los Angeles, John Espey Malibu, Penelope Gee, Sydney Australia, Vance Gerry Pasadena, G P Goold, South Hadley, Mass , Rinard Z Hart, Claremont David J Holmes Philadelphia, George Houle Los Angeles Sue A Kaplan, UCLA James E Lorson Fullerton Carol Morrison, Braille Institute, Los Angeles, Edward N O'Neil, Claremont, Stephen J Pigman, UCLA, Donald Tinker and Liza Walton, UCLA

He is further glad to record his gratitude to the following institutions for their kindnesses and courtesies British Library London, Bryn Mawr College Pennsylvania Case Western Reserve University Cleveland, Ohio Harvard University, Cambridge, Mass , the Library of Congress Washington, D C , Merton College, Oxford Pierpont Morgan Library, New York Princeton University New Jersey, Southern Illinois University, Carbondale, Trinity College Cambridge, the University Library Cambridge the University of San Francisco

INTRODUCTION

A CENTURY AGO, at the close of February 1896, *A Shropshire Lad* appeared The volume was published at the author's expense, it was received by critics with courtesy, and on occasion with enthusiasm, but it was not regarded as a work especially significant in English poetry The edition numbered about 500 copies, of which perhaps 154 were distributed in the United States, the book was priced two shillings six pence, it required more than two years for the edition to sell out [1]

The second edition, issued in 1898 at 3/6, likewise consisted only of about five hundred copies The third edition published in 1900 at 3/- each, numbered one thousand copies The fourth edition dated 1903 but published at the close of the previous year, consisted of two thousand copies at sixpence or a shilling, depending on format By the close of 1902, purchasers in Great Britain and the United States had acquired only two thousand copies The population of Great Britain was then in excess of 41,000,000, that of the United States, over 76,000 000 [1]

To keep prices down, the author, A E Housman, declined to accept royalties, a practice he continued for a quarter of a century At first, the poems only slowly attracted attention But, eventually, in World War I, they came to possess so solid a following that when Housman brought out his second book of verse, *Last Poems*, in 1922, it was regarded by many as the literary event of the year

Now, a hundred years after the original publication, new editions of *A Shropshire Lad* continue to be issued In 1990, Dover Thrift Editions produced a copy for a dollar, in the same year, the Tern Press published a limited edition with wood-engravings by Nicholas Parry In 1991, Walker Books issued an edition, with illustrations by Robin Bell Corfield, which was reprinted the following year Likewise in 1992, the Zauberberg Press in Kansas issued a very limited edition (twenty copies) with illustrations by John De Pol In 1994, Woodstock Books of Oxford and New York issued a facsimile of the first edition This brief catalogue, covering only 1990–1994, deliberately does not take into account reprints of Housman's *Collected Poems*

Alfred Edward Housman was born, on March 26, 1859, in a house called The Little Valley or The Valley House, Fockbury, in the parish of Catshill, Worcestershire [2,3] He was the eldest of the seven children of Edward Housman, a Bromsgrove solicitor, and his wife Sarah Jane Williams It was a talented family Clemence (1861-1955) is remembered as artist novelist and an active supporter of women's suffrage, Laurence (1865-1959), variously as illustrator novelist, playwright and likewise an active

---

1 For the size of the early editions and their prices, see Grant Richards *Housman 1897 1936* London 1941 (henceforth, Richards), pp 16, 25, 32 sq It is commonly and mistakenly, supposed that Henry Altemus issued an edition in Philadelphia in 1902 see Naiditch *Problems in the Life and Writings of A E Housman* Beverly Hills Krown & Spellman, 1995 (henceforth *PLW/AEH*), p 118 the earliest form of Altemus's text belongs to ca 1909

2 For his life, see A S F Gow's brief and excellent *A E Housman a Sketch* Cambridge 1936 for its defects some deliberate see Naiditch *A E Housman at University College London the Election of 1892*, Leiden E J Brill 1988 (henceforth, *AEH/UCL*) pp 11 26 sq and *PLW/AEH* p 227 See too especially *Classical Scholarship a Biographical Encyclopedia* edd W W Briggs Jr and W M Calder III New York Garland 1990, pp 190 204 (corrigenda *PLW/AEH* p ix n 2) and *The Letters of A E Housman* ed Henry Maas, London 1971 (henceforth, *Letters*) (with *PLW/AEH* pp 230 sq) Unfortunately, none of the formal biographies can be recommended without reservation although Norman Page's *A E Housman a Critical Biography* London 1985 (to be re issued in 1996) has merit it needs to be used with care (see *PLW/AEH* pp 231 sq)

3 Housman called it The Little Valley (H to unknown, Sept 30, 1930 Bryn Mawr College Adelman Collection) His family latterly called it The Valley House For the region see John Pugh, *Bromsgrove and the Housmans*, Bromsgrove 1974 (with *PLW/AEH* p 232)

supporter both of the women's rights movement and of pacifism Of the rest, Robert became a munitions expert, Basil a physician, Katharine Elizabeth wrote a history of the school where her husband, Edward W Symons had been headmaster, and George Herbert joined the army as an enlisted man and was killed in combat during the Boer War [4]

Housman's childhood was pleasant But about 1870 his mother developed cancer, dying the following year on his twelfth birthday, and this loss contributed to that dark view of existence that characterized him for the rest of his life It was indeed about this time that he abandoned Christianity not for agnosticism but for deism

By 1877, Housman stood at the head of his local school, King Edward VI Grammar School, Bromsgrove More significantly in the Oxford and Cambridge Schools Examination, he was ranked amongst the top twelve students nation-wide, earning distinction in Latin, Greek, French and History, in a field where 47% of the candidates did not pass at all [5] In this same year, he won a scholarship to St John's College, Oxford

At Oxford it cannot be said that Housman took his studies seriously To be sure, he received first class honors in Classical Moderations in 1879 But he also evidenced a cavalier attitude in his work, for example composing a poem for the Newdigate Prize the night before it was due In all probability he regarded himself as possessed of such talent and such genius that he had little need to apply himself to his studies In the event, in 1881, he was failed in his final examinations, a disgrace which caused him to withdraw into himself [6]

Housman had designed himself for the life of a scholar, and this failure at Oxford almost closed his career before it had properly begun With the reform of the Universities not long before, the chances for a failed candidate to obtain a college fellowship or a university professorship were greatly reduced, and this Housman must soon have realized He obtained a 'Pass' degree from Oxford, though with difficulty successfully took the Civil Service Examinations, albeit without special distinction, and, late in 1882 joined the Patent Office in London, probably first as the private secretary to the head of the Office His arrogance however soon lost him that appointment, and he became a higher division clerk in the Trade Marks Division This position Housman retained until 1892

Late in 1882, when he moved to London to work in the Patent Office, Housman dwelt with his Oxford friend, Moses John Jackson (1858-1923) in Bayswater lodgings Jackson, who had received first class honors in the Natural History examinations, now held a position as one of the twelve special "indexing clerks" in H M Patent Office Together with Jackson's brother Adalbert (died 1892) who was studying classics at University College, they lived together at least until late 1884 Around that time, Adalbert left London to work as a schoolmaster Not long afterwards, following an altercation, Jackson and Housman separated Jackson indeed already unhappy with administrative changes in the Patent Office in 1887 accepted a position as Principal of Sind College, Karachi and resigned from the

---

4 For Laurence see his autobiography *The Unexpected Years* Indianapolis 1936 There is no satisfactory biography albeit sufficient materials for a biography exist The chief modern study is Rodney Engen's *Laurence Housman* Stroud Catalpa Press 1983 For Clemence, there may be insufficient materials for a formal life Brief accounts of Housman's siblings appear in Pugh *Bromsgrove and the Housmans* pp lii-lxxiii

5 See *PLW/AEH* pp 4 6 7-8

6 For various explanations for Housman's failure see *AEH/UCL* pp 191 204 *PLW/AEH* pp 9-13 It was around this time that Housman became an atheist

Office His later efforts to return to London as a Professor of Physics at University College, London, though aided by Housman were unsuccessful

Jackson was Housman's greatest friend The altercation, the causes for which are uncertain was troubling, and the division between them was not healed for years Eventually, in 1900, Housman stood as godfather for the fourth of his friend's sons In the meanwhile, Housman, having taken rooms in Highgate, continued with his classical studies and, on the side began to compose poetry [7]

Housman's classical studies had begun in his childhood At Oxford, aside from his ordinary work, he spent considerable time and effort on the emendation of Propertius His first publication however concerned Horace, and it appeared while he was still technically an undergraduate It seems likely that, in sending an offprint of this paper to H A J Munro, Housman hoped that the former Professor of Latin at Cambridge would suggest a route by which he might escape the consequences of his failure at Oxford No such suggestion was forthcoming, the letters were merely polite [8] The following year 1883, Housman published a brief note on Ovid's *Ibis* Two years later, in 1885 he submitted a proposal for an edition, with commentary, of Propertius to the Oxford University Press, where it was rejected on Robinson Ellis's advice, and then to Macmillan's Ellis troubled to write a long letter to Housman, explaining the reasons for his rejection, Macmillan's declined it briefly and quickly [9] Housman however did not abandon a field which seemed closed to him Instead, he wrote a lengthy article "Emendationes Propertianae", dating it October 1886, and submitted it to the *Journal of Philology* the chief British classical periodical of the period The article was not only accepted but honored with primacy of place in the number when it appeared in 1887 [10] It was with this article that Housman began to regain the ground his Oxford failure had cost him The article attracted interest, and it was at this time that he gained the support of notable scholars such as R Y Tyrrell of Dublin Henry Jackson of Cambridge, and J P Postgate of both Cambridge and University College London Thereafter, Housman continued to compose technical papers, proposing corrections in major classical authors such as Horace and Ovid, Aeschylus and Sophocles and Euripides At length, in 1891, he completed a book, *The Manuscripts of Propertius* This he submitted to the Cambridge University Press It was rejected, though the Syndics of the Press recommended its inclusion as a series of articles in the *Journal of Philology* [11]

In 1892, when University College, London, advertised the positions of Professor of Latin and Professor of Greek, Housman was a candidate for either position, with a stated preference for the Chair of Latin His pamphlet of testimonials was, in rank of supporters and in the strength of their several commendations, outstanding, his publications, both by their excellence as critical essays and by the elegance of his exposition impressed the election committee, and despite his failure at Oxford the committee

7 For M J Jackson see *PLW/AEH* pp 132-144, for his brother Adalbert, see *ibid* pp 139 sq n 3 For the date of Housman's poetry, see *ibid* pp 103 sq

8 For dating of the lost correspondence with Munro, and its tone, see *ibid* pp 14-16

9 It is of course possible though perhaps less likely that Housman approached Macmillan s first For Housman and Ellis see *AEH/UCL* pp 32-52 Not improbably, it was Ellis who first turned Housman s interest to Propertius (*ibid* p 41) For Ellis's role in Oxford s refusal see Gilbert Murray *John O London's Weekly* 2, 1960, p 404 = *op cit* p 42

10 For the dating of this and others of Housman s classical papers see *PLW/AEH* pp 149-150

11 For Tyrrell, see *AEH/UCL* pp 216-220, for Jackson see *ibid* pp 165-172 for Postgate, see *ibid* pp 74-91 For the history of *The Manuscripts of Propertius* see *ibid* pp 77, 79

recommended the appointment of Housman to the position of his choice Thereafter, at University College, Housman fulfilled in exemplary fashion the duties assigned him [12]

In 1895, Housman found himself composing more and more poetry For much of his life, he had occasionally written verse, usually humorous, sometimes serious, but the new output differed in quality from most of what he had earlier achieved He himself attributed this poetical inspiration alternately to ill-health, a "relaxed sore throat" that afflicted him in the first five months of the year or to anxiety resulting from a controversy in which he was involved [13] In any event by the final months of 1895, he had enough to justify a volume

This book, which he entitled "Poems by Terence Hearsay', consisted of sixty-six poems, and differed from the final version It commenced with "The Recruit", later *A Shropshire Lad* III, and concluded with "Terence, this is stupid stuff", afterwards *ASL* LXII The volume was quickly declined by the publisher he approached [14] Housman reorganized the volume and, apparently at the suggestion of an Oxford friend, now of the British Museum library, he retitled it *A Shropshire Lad* His friend, A W Pollard, then arranged for the volume to be published, at Housman's expense, by Kegan Paul [15]

On its appearance *A Shropshire Lad* was fairly widely reviewed But few of the twenty-nine reviews and notices were in significant publications Apparently by accident, the book received no criticism in the *Athenaeum*, then the most influential literary weekly in Britain Even so, it attracted attention and enthusiasm both in England and in the United States [16] And two British publishers, John Lane and Grant Richards interested themselves in Housman Lane, who had purchased copies of the first edition and published them in the United States, probably sought to publish the author's next volume of verse, Richards seemingly expressed the desire to bring out a second edition In particularly seeking to reprint, rather than to issue a new work by the author, Richards was fortunate When the original publisher expressed no desire to reprint it, Housman transferred *A Shropshire Lad* to Richards In the years that followed, Richards brought out one inexpensive edition after another

Championed by William Archer in England and Witter Bynner in America, the latter of whom arranged for individual poems to be given a wider audience in *McClure's Magazine*, the book gradually became more and more popular Although the gradual increase in popularity of *A Shropshire Lad* is difficult to trace with precision, it is clear that, by 1922, Housman's standing as a poet with the population at large was high Although this afforded Housman satisfaction, he himself made no effort to "market" the volume It was rare for him to publish new poems in newspapers or periodicals He avoided interviews He did not encourage others to write about him, and there was little gossip to be found even in the literary periodicals His "trade" was that of professor of Latin, and the duties consequent to this position consumed much of his time, and whilst Housman ranks high as a poet the truth is that he ranks even higher as a classical scholar His principal work was an edition, with commentary, of the *Astronomica* by Marcus Manilius

It was around 1896 or 1897 that Housman began work on Manilius His first publication, a list of corrections in the first book, appeared in 1898, a second list in the fifth book, in 1900 Three years later,

---

12 For the election, see *AEH/UCL* pp 1-26 and relevant notes, for Housman at UCL, *ibid* pp 100-157

13 See *PLW/AEH* pp 86 89

14 For the Poems", see *PLW/AEH* pp 92 sq

15 For Pollard, see *AEH/UCL* pp 228-232

16 For the reception of Housman's verse see Philip Gardner, *A F Housman the Critical Heritage* London Routledge, 1992 with *PLW/AEH* pp 226 sq and Archie Burnett s review in *Essays in Criticism* 44 Jan 1994 pp 68-74

he published, again at his own expense, an edition of book one This, his first published classical book, appeared when he was forty-four It was a volume that excited both admiration and indignation Housman in his criticisms, had always been somewhat undiplomatic in his expressions of contempt, and his words often enough gave offence

> If I had no judgment and knew it and were nevertheless immutably resolved to edit a classic, I would single out my victim from the first of these three classes [authors surviving in one manuscript or in a few manuscripts closely derived from one] that would be best for the victim and best for me Authors surviving in a solitary MS are by far the easiest to edit, because their editor is relieved from one of the most exacting offices of criticism, from the balancing of evidence and the choice of variants They are the easiest, and for a fool they are the safest One field at least for the display of folly is denied him others are open, and in defending, correcting, and explaining the written text he may yet aspire to make a scarecrow of the author and a byword of himself, but with no variants to afford him scope for choice and judgment he cannot exhibit his impotence to judge and choose
>
> But the worst of having no judgment is that one never misses it and buoyantly embarks without it upon enterprises in which it is not so much a convenience as a necessity [17]

Nor did he limit himself to generalized criticisms His writings are replete with disagreeable comments on his predecessors and contemporaries "The worst of it" wrote Robinson Ellis, the author of *Noctes Manilianae*, "is that no one is exempted, the field is strewn with the corpses of his slain " Housman himself, remembering how he had treated Ellis in the book, added a note in one of his copies of the review Addressing Ellis, he remarked 'You are thank your stars' [18]

At the close of 1910 the Cambridge Professor of Latin, J E B Mayor died By this time, aside from hundreds of pages of occasional notes, articles and reviews, Housman had also edited Ovid's *Ibis* and Juvenal's satires for Postgate's *Corpus Poetarum Latinorum* and, as usual, at his own expense, brought out a separate edition of the satirist He was persuaded to stand for the Cambridge chair and, in 1911, he was elected [19] Additionally, he was then made a Fellow of Trinity College, Cambridge "The election of Mr A E Housman into the Professorship of Latin came as a surprise to all but a very few, but there were some who thought him the best Latinist in England and perhaps in Europe " So too his old Oxford college elected him to an Honorary Fellowship As a rule however Housman declined public honors By 1934, these included nine honorary doctorates and the Order of Merit The sole chief exception was his reluctant agreement to deliver the Leslie Stephen Lecture This lecture which he entitled *The Name and Nature of Poetry*, afforded him neither pleasure nor satisfaction though it was praised by many including T S Eliot Eliot's followers and admirers however, such as F R Leavis, thought they recognized in the talk an attack on their views [20]

---

17 *M Manilii astronomicon liber 1* London Grant Richards 1903 pp xxii sq xxxi

18 Ellis *Hermathena* 30 1904, p 7 Housman s annotated copy is at UCLA (PN2 H42) unfortunately on acquisition during World War II the notes were not recognized and the binder cropped them what remains is 'you are th[ ] | your stars

19 For Mayor see *AEH/UCL* pp 204 208 and *PLW/AEH* pp 32-34 For Housman s election to the Cambridge chair see *AEH/UCL* p 168 After Housman's appointment the chair was named the Kennedy Professorship (*PLW/AFH* pp 27 sq)

20 For the similarity of Housman and Eliot s views see B J Leggett, *The Poetic Art of A E Housman Theory and Practice*, Lincoln (Neb)/London University of Nebraska Press 1978, pp 87 sqq The first person to recognize their similarity seems to have been Abdul-Wahid Lulua in *A E Housman Critical Reputation 1896 1962*, Dissertation Case Western Reserve University 1962 p 88

During the last quarter century of his life, Housman edited the four remaining books of Manilius, and prepared an *editio minor* of that author he edited the *Bellum civile* of Lucan, and, on the invitation of the Cambridge University Press, prepared a second edition of Juvenal

In 1926, his edition of Lucan led scholars on the Continent to regard Housman as the leading Latinist in Great Britain In 1930, even though it was realized he would refuse, Housman was at least informally considered for the Poet Laureateship of Great Britain [21]

*   *   *

In the evening of April 30th, 1936 Housman died He was in his 78th year During his career as poet and scholar, many classicists had been angered by his criticisms, F R Leavis and his followers had been annoyed by his Leslie Stephen lecture, and many of the younger poets, identifying him with the older generation, were eager to discover reasons for denigrating and dismissing his work On the other hand, scholars specialising in verbal criticism and able to recognize ability and talent continued to think well of Housman's technical labors, and the public at large, charmed by his melodious verse, continued to purchase copy after copy of Housman s poetry But ammunition against him was provided at once to classical scholars, literary critics, and poets by his brother Laurence

Housman s will included the clause "I direct my brother, Laurence Housman, to destroy all my prose manuscripts in whatever language, and I permit him but do not enjoin him to select from my verse manuscript writing, and to publish, any poems which appear to him to be completed and to be not inferior to the average of my published poems, and I direct him to destroy all other poems and fragments of verse" These instructions, naturally addressed to a relative, were badly carried out

In composing a memoir, Laurence included extracts from his brother's classical notebooks, misrepresenting them as generalized attacks awaiting a victim "If we all knew as little as ___ does, we should doubtless find the classics as easy as he does " "Nature not content with denying to Mr ___ the faculty of thought, has endowed him with the faculty of writing " "When ___ has acquired a scrap of misinformation he cannot rest till he has imparted it " This revelation damaged Housman's reputation for honesty and it played into the hands of those who, preferring literary to textual studies, were troubled because Housman had publicly affirmed that literary critics worthy of the title were extraordinarily rare [22] And those who had not dared to attack Housman whilst he was alive, or who had been bloodied by him in controversy, were now given ample opportunity to signal their dislike and safely to record their disdain [23]

---

21 For his rank on the Continent, see A Bierl/W M Calder III/R L Fowler *The Prussian and the Poet the Letters of Ulrich von Wilamowitz-Moellendorff to Gilbert Murray*, Berlin Weidmann, 1991, p 124 with note 553, cf *op cit* p 67 For the possibility of his becoming Laureate, see H W Garrod to Nichol Smith, Apr 27, 1930 (Merton College, Oxford Garrod Papers 1 45 p 4) See also *Letters* p 296

22 For Housman's sentences", see Naiditch, ' The Slashing Style that All Know and Few Applaud the Invective of A E Housman in *The Greenbank Colloquium on the History of English Classical Scholarship* ed H D Jocelyn (forthcoming), for Notebooks A, X and Y, see *PLW/AEH* pp 106-113 For this clause of the will, see L Housman in A E Housman, *More Poems*, London Cape 1936 p 7

23 I adopt the suggestion of E N O'Neil (in conversation 1971/72 *per lit* Oct 20 1995)

With regard to the verse, Laurence relied not on his brother's will but on his memory of a conversation "he said he wished me to include nothing which I considered inferior to anything that had already appeared I did not then admit to him that the inclusion in *A Shropshire Lad* of a poem which I thought inferior to the rest would make my task easier than it might otherwise have been' The result was that poems were published which Housman would not have cared to see in print and personal information made public which perhaps, Housman had never meant to disclose [24]

And the nature of some of the poems led many critics to center their attention not on the merits or defects of the verse but on their purportedly autobiographical nature [25]

The result was that, for many literary critics and for some classical scholars, Housman's work fell from favor, and, for a quarter of a century, scholars and teachers—though not the public at large—ceased to hold his writings in esteem But, especially from the early 1960s, a resurgence of interest took place in Great Britain and, not much later in the United States In 1961, John Carter brought out *A E Housman Selected Prose* In 1966, Tom Burns Haber *The Making of A Shropshire Lad* and, the following year, a popular account of Housman for the Twayne series In 1971, Rupert Hart-Davis and Harvard University Press published *The Letters of A E Housman* in 1972, the Cambridge University Press, *The Classical Papers of A E Housman*, and, in 1973, a Housman Society was brought into existence [26]

Since then several biographies of Housman have appeared as well as books on his verse In addition there have been twenty-one volumes of the *Housman Society Journal*, four volumes of the Japanese *A E Housman Journal*, a massive attempt to trace the "Critical Heritage from 1896 to 1951, and, of course, numerous reprints of Housman's *Collected Poems* and *A Shropshire Lad*

---

24 Laurence had quickly decided that there were sufficient materials to publish (LH to W Rothenstein May 12 1936 Harvard University, Houghton Library, bMs 1148 741 15) He had a typescript transcription made of complete, or nearly complete poems and consulted others as to their merit (For a copy of the typescript, see Trinity College, Cambridge Add Ms b 120) Laurence, endeavoring to follow instructions then disbound the four manuscript notebooks, discarded all pages only with unpublished matter and cutting up the remainder pasted it onto sheets These fragments he then sold for £2 000 to Scribner s whence it was obtained by the bookseller B J Beyer for $13,500, who sold it to Mrs Matthew John Whittall apparently for $40,000 Mrs Whittall donated it to the Library of Congress There for purposes of preservation, the fragments were remounted Not long after T Burns Haber misled Laurence into supposing he had lost his control over the publication of the fragments and published them himself as *The Manuscript Poems of A E Housman* For the fate of the Notebooks see J Carter *Book Collector* 4 Summer 1955, pp 110-114 D A Randall *Dukedom Large Enough*, New York 1969, pp 162-165 Aside from the manuscripts in the Library of Congress a few survive in the Adelman Collection, Bryn Mawr College, and in the Pierpont Morgan Library New York

With regard to Housman's prose writings, Laurence authorised the preservation of the Cambridge lectures (University Library Cambridge Add Mss 6874-6902) for Gow had advised him of the author s verbal decision to allow their survival Further Laurence had typescripts prepared of the lectures Housman had delivered to the UCL Literary Society and gave private readings then he undertook to destroy them One lecture, on Swinburne was accidentally preserved and eventually published reprinted in A E Housman *Collected Poems and Selected Prose* ed C Ricks, London Penguin 1988 (see *AEH/UCL* pp 150-156) Housman considered depositing in the British Museum an autobiographical note not to be seen for fifty years (*Letters* p 348)

25 See Randy Lynn Meyer, *A E Housman and the Critics* Dissertation University of Toledo (Ohio), 1994 (summary in *DAI-A55108* Feb 1995 p 2407 [CD-ROM])

26 For the Classical Papers, see *PLW/AEH* pp 145-50, for some of the biographies see *ibid* pp 180-194 For *A E Housman the Critical Heritage* ed P Gardner London/New York Routledge 1992 see above footnote 16

A SELECTION OF EARLY AND ILLUSTRATED EDITIONS OF A SHROPSHIRE LAD

Case 1

The number of copies in the earliest editions of *A Shropshire Lad* ordinarily was small 500 copies 1000 copies, 2000 copies and the like In Great Britain, it was Grant Richards who by bringing out numerous editions, kept the work before the public at large For the American market, John Lane at first purchased sheets of British editions, then, in 1906, he had a large number of copies printed These he issued periodically over the next nine years Because *A Shropshire Lad* was not copyrighted in the United States, others began to reprint it Mosher in 1906, Kennerley in 1907, Altemus around 1909 etc [27]

The earliest "limited", fine-press edition of *A Shropshire Lad* appeared in Maine in 1906 the earliest illustrated edition by William Hyde, in 1908 the first British limited edition, produced by the Riccardi Press, in 1914 It was probably in 1919 that the first text printed with a preface was published, the preface having been composed by William Stanley Braithwaite, an African-American poet and critic

(1) *A Shropshire Lad* by A F Housman London Kegan Paul Trench Trubner, & Co Ltd 1896 Label A **First Edition, first label, signed by the author, who has added two changes he had introduced into the second 1923 edition One of about 350 copies, 250 with Label A This work quickly won the regard of many critics, writers and ordinary readers with poems such as the fortieth

> Into my heart an air that kills
> From yon far country blows
> What are those blue remembered hills
> What spires what farms are those?
>
> That is the land of lost content,
> I see it shining plain,
> The happy highways where I went
> And cannot come again

In 1896 the London *Times* reviewer awarded *A Shropshire Lad* a brief, favorable notice concluding Mr Housman has a true sense of the sweetness of country life and of its tragedies too, and his gift of melodious expression is genuine The *Academy* reviewer declared *A Shropshire Lad* to be "a book that has a hundred claims upon the love of all who are the sincere servants of Poetry' Willa Cather observed 'There is something which makes Mr Housman different from the poets of the time and sets him quite apart, I should say that is largely because he is simply a singer ' [28]

UCLA Special Collections PR 4809 H15s From the Library of Majl and Carmelita Rosecrans Ewing

---

27 For the date of Altemus s first edition usually assigned to ca 1902 see above footnote 1

28 [Thomas Humphry Ward] *Times* March 27 1896 p 13d reprinted in *A L Housman the Critical Heritage* ed P Gardner London Routledge 1992 p 58 Norman Gale *Academy* I, July 11, 1896, p 30 = Gardner pp 68 sq Cather *The Home Monthly* Oct 1897 = *The World and the Parish* ed W M Curtin Lincoln (Neb) 1970 p 358 = *PLH/AEH* p 98

(2) *A Shropshire Lad* by A E Housman, New York John Lane, The Bodley Head 1897 Label B, accompanied by Van der Weyde photograph of ca 1894, signed **First Edition, with cancel titleleaf, signed by the author Late in 1896, Kegan Paul had the other half of the edition bound, selling some 154 or 162 copies to John Lane with a cancel titleleaf giving his name as publisher in New York [29]

Private Collection From the Library of Perry Molstad

(3) *A Shropshire Lad* by A E Housman, London Grant Richards, 1898 **Second Edition One of about 500 copies Richards has recorded his memory of his negotiations with Housman (*Housman 1897-1936*, London 1941, p 24)

> I recall Housman as having repeated that I might produce the second edition of his book and myself as having remonstrated with him about his refusal to take any share of the profits that in my opinion were sure to accrue to its publisher ' The book will become better and better known It won't take over two years to sell the second edition There is bound later on to be a big profit " Housman's reply was to the point "I am not a poet by trade I am a professor of Latin I do not wish to make profit out of my poetry It is not my business

Richards follows his account with the story that McClure's in America had sent Housman cheques to reprint his poems, and these Housman returned That story, whilst essentially true, is here anachronistic it was only later that McClure's sent payment For his part, Housman was pleased with the sales of the second edition, albeit his instructions concerning its printing were ignored ' The second edition" he wrote to Paul Lemperly "contains nothing new except a few misprints" (first printed, A E Newton, *This Book-Collecting Game*, Boston 1928, p 254, for reprints, see *HSJ* 17, 1991, p 44)

Private Collection From the Library of Lydia Scott (April 1899)

(4) *A Shropshire Lad* by A E Housman, London Grant Richards, 1900 **Third Edition One of about 1000 copies, albeit few copies have survived

Private Collection

(5) *A Shropshire Lad* by A E Housman London Grant Richards, 1903 **Fourth Edition, issued at the close of 1902 in some 2000 copies

Private Collection

(6) *A Shropshire Lad* by A E Housman, London Grant Richards 1904 ("The Smaller Classics") **Fifth Edition, offered in two formats (in leather a shilling in cloth six pence) the last edition printed by Richards before his first bankruptcy To the firm which purchased the business, Housman wrote concerning this edition [30]

> Mr Grant Richards included my book *A Shropshire Lad* in his series of The Smaller Classics without consulting me, and to my annoyance I contented myself with remonstrating, and did not demand its withdrawal, but now that I have the chance I take it and I refuse to allow the book to be any

29 For the statistics see Naiditch, "The First Edition of *A Shropshire Lad* in Bookshop and Auction Room *Housman New Perspectives* edd A Holden/R Birch London Macmillan (forthcoming) n 8

30 H to Messrs Alexander Moring Aug 17 1906 Richards p 73 *Letters* p 87

longer included in the series I hope that you will not be very much aggrieved, but I think it unbecoming that the work of a living author should appear under such a title

Private Collection

(7) *A Shropshire Lad* by A E Housman New York John Lane Company, The Bodley Head, 1906 **The First American Edition, with '*The* | BODLEY | HEAD" at foot of spine The copy on exhibition is the one that, by its ownership inscription, establishes this printing as the first

When I was one-and-twenty
  I heard a wise man say,
Give crowns and pounds and guineas
  But not your heart away,
Give pearls away and rubies
  But keep your fancy free '
But I was one-and-twenty,
  No use to talk to me

When I was one-and-twenty
  I heard him say again
The heart out of the bosom
  Was never given in vain
'Tis paid with sighs a plenty
  And sold for endless rue '
And I am two-and-twenty
  And oh 'tis true 'tis true
        A Shropshire Lad XIII

Private Collection From the Library of Esther Everett Lafe (June 1906) [31]

(8) *A Shropshire Lad* by A E Housman, London E Grant Richards, 1907 **Seventh Edition

Private Collection From the Library of Perry Molstad

(9) *A Shropshire Lad* by A E Housman with a Preface by William Stanley Braithwaite, Boston The Four Seas Company, 1919 **Second impression [32]

Private collection

ILLUSTRATED EDITIONS

Efforts to illustrate Housman reach back to 1908 In that year, at the publisher's desire, William Hyde prepared a series of color-illustrations They failed to please the author The next major attempt to illustrate *A Shropshire Lad* was by Claud Lovat Fraser It left so much to be desired that Housman declined to let it appear with his text

Probably the most successful attempt at illustration was that by Agnes Miller Parker in Harrap's 1940 edition The poems, having a rustic element, arguably call for a generally rough form of technique, such as woodcut On the other hand, the polished nature of Housman's verse requires more sophisticated an art-form Apparently alive to these issues, Parker prepared wood-engravings

To date, nearly thirty artists, including Joan Hassall and Paul Landacre, John De Pol and James Thurber have undertaken to illustrate individual poems or whole works [33]

---

31 For the first American printing see *PIW/AFH* p 118

32 For Braithwaite, see W H Robinson, *Dictionary of Literary Biography* 54 1 Detroit Gale Research Co , 1987 pp 3-12

33 For Housman on Hyde see *Letters* index with Richards index Hyde's original blocks are preserved at Southern Illinois University Carbondale For Housman on Fraser, see *Letters* index with Richards index Fraser's originals are at Bryn Mawr College For a list of artists see *PLW/AEH* p 210 n 2

(10) *A Shropshire Lad* by A E Housman, with Eight Illustrations in Colour by William Hyde, London Grant Richards, [1908] **First illustrated edition

Private Collection

(11) *A Shropshire Lad by A E Housman* Illustrations by Elinore Blaisdell, New York Illustrated Editions Company, [1932] **Apparently, the earliest publication of the Blaisdell illustrations Frontispiece, colored, depicting "The True Lover" (*ASL* LIII) Housman, influenced by the Scottish ballads describes a woman who, having rejected her lover, discovers herself compelled to come to him at his call, and they embrace [34]

> "Oh lad, what is it lad, that drips
>   Wet from your neck on mine?
> What is it falling on my lips,
>   My lad, that tastes of brine?"
>
> "Oh, like enough 'tis blood, my dear,
>   For when the knife has slit
> The throat across from ear to ear
>   'Twill bleed because of it "

Private Collection

(12) A E Housman *A Shropshire Lad* Decorations by Edw A Wilson, New York The Heritage Press, 1935 **Frontispiece initialed by artist The earliest edition of Wilson's illustrations, which were reissued in 1938 and again in 1951

Private Collection

(13) *A Shropshire Lad* by A E Housman With Wood Engravings by Agnes Miller Parker, London etc George G Harrap & Co Ltd, 1940 **First Parker edition Illustrating "The Recruit" (*ASL* III), the poem Housman originally intended to begin his book

Private Collection From the Library of Perry Molstad For the placement of "The Recruit" in *Poems by Terence Hearsay* see *PLH/AEH* pp 92 sq

(14) *A Shropshire Lad* by A E Housman Illustrations by Piers Browne, Southampton Ashford Press, 1988 **Foreword by Kingsley Amis On display, the illustration to 'Loveliest of trees"

> Loveliest of trees the cherry now
> Is hung with bloom along the bough,
> And stands about the woodland ride
> Wearing white for Eastertide
>
> Now, of my threescore years and ten,
> Twenty will not come again,
> And take from seventy springs a score,
> It only leaves me fifty more

> And since to look at things in bloom
> Fifty springs are little room,
> About the woodlands I will go
> To see the cherry hung with snow
>
>   *A Shropshire Lad* II

Private Collection

---

34 For dating of this edition see Naidlitch in *Housman New Perspectives* edd A Holden/R Birch London Macmillan (forthcoming) n 33

LIMITED EDITIONS AND PRIVATE PRINTINGS
OF A SHROPSHIRE LAD

Case 2

Housman took no pleasure in limited editions, for these by their nature, are designed to frustrate the advantage printing has over reproducing books in manuscript Nor was he ordinarily impressed with bibliophiles, whom he once described as an "idiotic class", a criticism directed at book-collectors whose interest centered not on the content of books but rather on their form But his friends and acquaintances included several book-collectors, presumably excluded from the general condemnation, because they were scholars in their own right A W Pollard (Keeper of Printed Books in the British Museum) Ingram Bywater (sometime Regius Professor of Greek at Oxford), and Sir Stephen Gaselee (Librarian of the House of Lords) Although Housman regarded a correct text as a book's chief merit, it would be wrong to pretend that he was entirely indifferent to type or margins or paper or bindings These he regarded as useful in making a book readable and therefore of ancillary value

(15) *A Shropshire Lad* by A E Housman Portland (Maine) Thomas B Mosher 1906 ** The Second American Edition, first Mosher Edition, limited to 925 copies This printing appears in a variety of formats In 1913, and again in 1922, Mosher reprinted the text

Private Collection

(16) *A Shropshire Lad* by A E Housman, London Philip Lee Warner, Publisher to the Medici Society Ld 1914 ** The Riccardi Edition No 4 of 1000 copies on paper, twelve copies also were printed on vellum

Private Collection

(17) *A Shropshire Lad* by A E Housman, [Chipping Campden The Alcuin Press, 1929] **No 320 of 325 copies

Private Collection See below footnote 38

(18) A E Housman *A Shropshire Lad* with Illustrations by Patrick Procktor, London The Folio Society, 1986

Private Collection

(19) A E Housman, *A Shropshire Lad* with wood-engravings by Nicholas Parry, [Market Drayton Shropshire] The Tern Press 1990 **No 65 of 225 copies

Private Collection

(20) *A Shropshire Lad* by A E Housman Wood engravings by John De Pol, Coffeyville The Zauberberg Press 1992 **The colophon reads 'THIS BOOK is one of twenty copies printed by hand on The Perfidious Albion, No 7039, built by the printer The type face is Lutetia 14 D set with arthritic hands, and printed on dampened Rives, from France, and five copies on Chilham the final handmade

from Barcham-Green No comma, nor emendation, has been offered by the scrofulous printer Designed, edited, printed & bound, by D von R Drenner"

(21) 'The Merry Guide" (*ASL* XLII), New York The Unbound Anthology, The Poets' Guild, [ca 1930?]

(22) "The Carpenter's Son" (*ASL* XLVII), Los Angeles 1931 **Seemingly the only copy known

(23) "On the idle hill of summer" (*ASL* XXXV) Printed by D Tinker Feb 1985 **One of five copies

(24) "With Rue My Heart is Laden' and "Into My Heart", [Pasadena] The Weatherbird Press, [ca 1991] **Printed by Vance Gerry with wood-engravings by Thomas Bewick

With rue my heart is laden   By brooks too broad for leaping
For golden friends I had   The lightfoot boys are laid
For many a rose-lipt maiden   The rose-lipt girls are sleeping
And many a lightfoot lad   In fields where roses fade

A Shropshire Lad LIV

A SELECTION OF EDITIONS OF LAST POEMS
AND RELATED MATTER

(25) *Last Poems* by A E Housman, London Grant Richards, 1922 **First Edition One of 34 copies sent as gifts on the author's instructions The present copy was sent to John Masefield, later the Poet Laureate

(26) *Last Poems* by A E Housman, London Grant Richards, 1922 **First Edition

The sigh that heaves the grasses
Whence thou wilt never rise
Is of the air that passes
And knows not if it sighs
The diamond tears adorning
Thy low mound on the lea,
Those are the tears of mourning,
That weeps, but not for thee

Last Poems XXVII

POPULARITY

Housman's verse was slow to become popular But his melodious verse, combined with its military theme, bleak realism and individualistic, courageous outlook, appealed to many during the first World War and after With the publication of *Last Poems* in 1922, Housman's popularity rose In this period, tens of thousands of copies of his poems were printed and sold The price of the first edition of *A Shropshire Lad* which had only been four pounds in 1919, reached $157 50 in 1923 and, by 1929, $625 00 It was in this period lovers of poetry began regularly to write to Housman Of course, earlier, admirers had communicated with him

In 1897, an unknown correspondent began to send him good wishes on his birthday, in 1902, Willa Cather made an unannounced visit to his home in Highgate, London, in 1903, Witter Bynner began his long correspondence with Housman Housman was, despite his reserve and reluctance to meet new people, amenable to giving pleasure to others by acquiescing in undemanding requests, and he could be charming to those who approached him in the right manner Thus, to one he wrote "My heart always warms to people who do not come to see me, especially Americans, to whom it seems to be more of an effort, and your preference of the Cam to the Hudson, which I have always understood to be one of the finest rivers, is also an ingratiating trait If you think this note a reward I shall be pleased "[35]

In the later 1920s, when his reputation was highest, he was almost beset by admirers Some, like John Sparrow and John Carter and Houston Martin and Seymour Adelman, approached him openly Some, like Charles Wilson, wrote in order to obtain letters to sell, at least one, James George ("Alfred Housman") Leippert, used subterfuge to elicit responses [36]

(27) Letter to Mr Melvutsky

Trinity College
Cambridge
England
18 Dec 1929

Dear Mr Melvutsky

I think Mr Rubin asked me the same question, and I replied that authors do not know which are their best works and therefore had better not have opinions on the subject If you prefer *Last Poems* you agree with Masefield and Mrs Wharton

Yours sincerely

A E Housman

UCLA Special Collections Ms 100 box 45 Melvutsky and Arnold Rubin (who corresponded with Housman from 1928 to 1932) are unknown

---

35 See L Housman, *A E H* London 1937 pp 136 sq and *Letters* pp 47 sq , I conjecture that this individual learnt Housman s birthday from the 1897 *Who s Who* F K Brown/Leon Edel, *Willa Cather* 1953 New York Avon 1980 index *Thirty Housman Letters to Witter Bynner* ed T B Haber New York 1957 H to Neilson Abeel Oct 4 1935 Abeel *Forum and Century* 96, Oct 1936 p 192 *Letters* p 377 I have altered the paragraphing

36 For Charles Wilson, see my commendation of Henry Maas at *PLWALH* pp 161 sq For the exposure of Leippert, see *ibid* pp 39-41

(28) Cutting of the first printing of "Epitaph on an Army of Mercenaries", the London *Times* Oct 31, 1917, p 7

> These in the day when heaven was falling,   Their shoulders held the sky suspended,
>   The hour when earth's foundations fled   They stood, and earth's foundations stay
> Followed their mercenary calling   What God abandoned, these defended
>   And took their wages and are dead   And saved the sum of things for pay
>
>   *Last Poems* XXXVII

Private Collection

POSTHUMOUSLY PUBLISHED VERSE

Case 3

Following his brother's death, Laurence quickly concluded that there were sufficient materials to publish a new volume He had a typescript transcription made of complete or nearly complete, poems, and consulted G M Trevelyan, F L Lucas and A S F Gow as to their merit, and he then made a selection published as *More Poems* The following year, Laurence ignored the advice he had earlier solicited and published all of the remaining poems and principal fragments, save one in his memoir as "Additional Poems" The notebooks themselves, Laurence partly destroyed, selling the remainder to Scribner's [37]

(29) [John Carter,] *The Poetical Manuscripts of A E Housman* (Annotated typescript draft) **The final version of Carter's analysis accompanied the fragmentary notebooks to New York and, eventually, to the Library of Congress The present draft has been annotated by Carter and especially by David Randall, both then of Scribner's

     Private Collection From the Library of P B Morris

(30) *More Poems* by A E Housman, London Jonathan Cape, [1936] **Duplicate Proof for Retention dated 'Oct 16"

     Private Collection The actual marked proof itself survives in the Adelman Collection, Bryn Mawr College Pennsylvania (R.B R PR 4809 H15 A68 1936), another unmarked proof exists in another private collection

(31) *More Poems* by A E Housman, London Jonathan Cape [1936] **No 284 of 379 copies

> I to my perils   The thoughts of others
>   Of cheat and charmer   Were light and fleeting,
>   Came clad in armour   Of lovers' meeting
>   By stars benign   Or luck or fame
> Hope lies to mortals   Mine were of trouble,
>   And most believe her   And mine were steady
>   But man's deceiver   So I was ready
>   Was never mine   When trouble came
>
>   *More Poems* VI

Private Collection

---

37 For the disposal of the Notebooks, see above, footnote 24

(32) *Stars* [by] A E Housman, Paris [Imprimerie du Trocadéro,] 1969 **This reprint of *More Poems* VII is lettered "X" and is one of ten copies, signed by Frederic Prokosch Prokosch, a noted novelist, had had small editions of individual poems printed, with false dates, then sold them In the present copy the place and date of printing are on a cancel covering the false imprint "Venice 1939" His imposture was exposed in September 1972, and as evidence of repentance, he pasted on correction slips [37] Later, from 1982-1984, Prokosch issued very limited editions of individual poems, which he copied by hand on printed forms These included poems such as Housman's "Loveliest of trees" Each appeared in an edition of five under the imprint of the Prometheus Press

Private Collection

(33) *Collected Poems* by A E Housman, London Jonathan Cape, 1939 **First Edition (second state), edited by John Carter [39] Housman strongly objected to the idea that *A Shropshire Lad* and *Last Poems* should be bound together Indeed, when he received a press-cutting from the *New York Times* implying that such had been done by the authorized American publisher, he wrote to the Society of Authors to see whether he could force them to withdraw the volume In the event, the rumor was false During Housman's lifetime, two editions included both books In 1929, H P R Feinberg was allowed to publish a fine-press edition of both books at the Alcuin Press, and deliberately flouted Housman's wishes by issuing some of his copies in a single volume The Braille edition likewise brought the two volumes together [40]

After Housman's death, since his principal poems had appeared in four different volumes, Laurence decided to allow his poetry to be brought together in one volume Since 1939, Housman's *Collected Poems* has likewise remained continuously in print both in the United States and in Great Britain

Private Collection

CLASSICAL STUDIES

Case 4

'It seems hardly fair that the same man should be such a scholar and such a poet '[41] Housman's standing as a classical scholar is higher even than his standing as a poet As a scholar, he is regarded as one of the three greatest classicists in the history of Great Britain This was indicated for example, by C O Brink in his book *English Classical Scholarship Historical Reflections on Bentley, Porson and Housman*, only a decade ago

Following his failure at Oxford, Housman divided his time about equally between problems in Greek and Latin With his appointment to the Latin Chair at University College, he began to limit himself almost entirely to Latin writers from Lucretius to Juvenal

38 See Nicolas Barker *The Butterfly Books*, London Bertram Rota 1987 pp 173-75 230

39 The first state seems to survive only in two copies the copyright volume in the British Library Carter's own copy at the Lilly Library

40 See AEH to Holt Jan 4, 1925, Holt to Housman Jan 16, 1925; H to Holt, Feb 2, 1925 Princeton University, New Jersey Henry Holt Archive LH to H Thring, Jan 12 and 16 1925 *Letters* pp 225 sq For the ordinary Alcuin edition see above no 17 for a copy of the Braille edition, see the William White Collection University of Virginia Charlottesville

41 J D Duff to E H Blakeney March 16, 1931 British Library Add Ms 18980 ft 57 sq = *PLH/AEH* pp 46 sq

(34) Draft notes for a letter on the Corpus Tibullianum Undated, and without clear and certain means available for assigning to a particular year The handwriting seems to belong to the first decade of the twentieth century Possibly sent to J P Postgate (1853/1926) [42] Two extracts are provided

<I 4> 81 *heu heu* is at any rate as old as Virgil's cod Romanus but the prevalence of *heu heu* in the late and bad MSS of Tibullus and the way it dwindles and gives place to *eheu* when you ascend to older and better MSS like Ovid's and Horace's, is striking and I think significant Then look at passages like Prop II 24 20 sq , Sil XI 212, Stat Ach I 68 where the best or best-spelling MSS give *eheu* and others have *heu heu* Even in Tibullus we once find *heheu*, which may be a true form as it occurs in the Palatine of Virgil buc 8 58 and in several other places

III 6 19-21 *siqua est* is right I think In praying a god not to do hurt to you it was usual to suggest that he should hurt some one [*sic*] else because gods being what they are they can hardly be expected to be happy unless they are hurting somebody Lygdamus recommends Bacchus to persecute his old enemy Agaue, but hints rather humorously that there may be no such person Propertius III 24 19 expresses similar doubt about Mens Bona

UCLA Special Collecions coll 1501 box 1 folder 5 (Mayl Ewing)

(35) Letter to Robinson Ellis (1834/1913) [43]

University of London
University College
1 May 1907

Dear Mr Ellis,

 Loewe's collation of the cod Matr M 31 of Manilius has been sent over from Goettingen and is now in the library of this college, where it will remain till midsummer I send you word of this in case you may wish to consult it or I should be very pleased to give you any information about it

   I am yours very truly

    A E Housman

UCLA Special Collections Ms 100 box 45 From the Library of C K Ogden

(36) Postcard to Stephen Gaselee (1882/1943), of Magdalene College Cambridge

What I should have said and thought I was saying is that the hiatus of monosyllables occurs only in the 2nd syllable of the dactyl and that *in that place* the hiatus of words other than monosyllables does not occur – the only exceptions being in proper names *Panopeae et, Ennii insignis* Hiatus like *etesiae esse* occurs even where there is no Greek word *uale inquit* and probably Lucr 6 743 *remigi oblitae*

        Yrs

12 Feb 1913
          A E Housman

UCLA Special Collections Ms 100 box 72

---

[42] For Housman and Postgate see *AEH/UCL* pp 74-91, *PIW/AEH* pp 217 220

[43] For Housman and Ellis see *AEH/UCL* pp 32-52 *PLW/ALII* pp 216 219 Ellis had published extensive if inaccurate, extracts from the codex Matritensis of Manilius

(37) Offprint of A E Housman's "The Manuscripts of Propertius", *Journal of Philology* 21, 1892, pp 101-160 **In 1891, whilst still a clerk at the Patent Office, Housman completed a critical work called *The Manuscripts of Propertius* With Postgate as sponsor, he submitted it to the Cambridge University Press The Syndics of the Press declined it, recommending instead that it be published as a series of articles in the *Journal of Philology* [44] After Housman's death, his friend and colleague A S F Gow gave away his offprints

UCLA Special Collections PA 6141 H817a v 1

(38) A E Housman, edition of Ovid's "Ibis" *Corpus Poetarum Latinorum* ed I P Postgatius, Londinii sumptibus G Bell et filiorum, 1894 **First edition Late in 1891, Postgate entrusted Housman with the task of editing Ovid's Ibis, and this work, Housman's first published edition of a classical text, duly appeared three years later [45]

Private Collection

(39) *Cornelii Taciti historiarum libri qui supersunt The Histories of Tacitus with Introduction, Notes and an Index by the Rev W A Spooner*, London Macmillan and Co , 1891 **In 1892, Housman was elected to the Latin chair at University College, London This book was one he used in teaching It was his custom to mark in the margins the names of the students on whom he meant to call to translate and to parse In the present book appear the names of his students Gerald Gould, the poet, and Annette M B Meakin, latterly a traveller and writer

Private Collection

(40) *M Manilii astronomicon liber primus* recensuit et enarrauit A E Housman London Grant Richards, 1903 **First edition One of 400 copies Label B [46] This, Housman's first printed classical book, was (as usual) published at his own expense

UCLA Special Collections 84563 v 1 From the libraries of Robinson Ellis, Stephen Gaselee, and C K Ogden

(41) Robinson Ellis, review of Housman's edition of Manilius book I, *Hermathena* 30, 1904, pp 1-14

UCLA Special Collections PN 2 H42 vol 30

(42) *D Iunii Iuuenalis satuae* editorum in usum A E Housman, Londinii apud E Grant Richards, 1905 **First separate edition One of 400 copies Like the Manilius before it, the Juvenal includes much trenchant criticism of Housman's contemporaries

A hundred years ago it was their rule to count the MSS and trust the majority But this pillow was snatched from under them by the great critics of the 19th century and the truth that MSS must be weighed not counted is now too widely known to be ignored The sluggard has lost his pillow but he has kept his nature and must needs find something else to loll on so he fabricates, to suit the change of season his precious precept of following one MS wherever possible Engendered by infirmity and designed for comfort, no wonder if it misses the truth at which it was never aimed

---

44 For the history of the book see *AEH/UCL* p 77 This first article is usually misdated 1893 see *PLW/AEH* p 149
45 For the date of the assignment see *PLW/AEH* pp 73 sq
46 The earlier label see *PLW/AEH* pp 119-121 For Housman's Manilius, see G P Goold in *A E Housman New Perspectives* edd Birch and Holden London Macmillan (forthcoming)

Its aim was purely humanitarian to rescue incompetent editors alike from the toil of editing and from the shame of acknowledging that they cannot edit

Private Collection

(42) *M Annaei Lucani belli ciuilis libri decem* editorum in usum edidit A E Housman, Oxonii apud Basilium Blackwell, 1926 **First edition

(43) *Thesaurus linguae Latinae* vol I fasc V, Lipsiae in aedibus B G Teubneri, 1902, column 966 **Housman had little respect for this dictionary In 1911, concerning a lexicographer who followed the current fashionable text of Juvenal, he remarked [47]

Who was the first and chief Latin writer to use the Greek word for a cat αἰλουρος ?[48] The answer to this question can be found in many Latin dictionaries, but not in the latest and most elaborate The five greatest universities of Germany have combined their resources to produce a *thesaurus linguae Latinae*, whose instalments, published during the last 12 years, run to 6000 pages, and have brought it down to the letter D The part containing *aelurus* appeared in 1902 it cites the word from Gellius, from Pelagius, and from the so-called Hyginus but it does not cite it from the 15th satire of Juvenal Here we find illustrated a theme on which historians and economists have often dwelt the disadvantage of employing slave-labour In Germany in 1902 the inspired text of Juvenal was the text of Buecheler's second edition That edition was published in the last decade of the 19th century, when the tide of obscurantism, now much abated was at its height, and when the cheapest way to win applause was to reject emendations which everyone had hitherto accepted and to adopt lections from the MSS which no one had yet been able to endure Buecheler riding on the crest of the wave had expelled from the text the conjecture as it then was *aeluros*, and restored the *caeruleos* of the MSS That was enough for the chain-gangs working at the dictionary in the ergastulum at Munich theirs not to reason why That every other editor for the last three centuries, and that Buecheler himself in his former edition, had printed *aeluros* they consigned to oblivion they provided this vast and expensive lexicon with an article on *aelurus* in which Juvenal's name did not occur [49] Everyone can figure to himself the mild inward glow of pleasure and pride which the author of this unlucky article felt while he was writing it and the peace of mind with which he said to himself, when he went to bed that night, 'Well done thou good and faithful servant '[50]

Private Collection From the library of A S F Gow (1887-1978)

47 *D Iunii Iuuenalis saturae* Edidit in usum editorum A E Housman, 1931 Cambridge 1956, pp lv sq Housman declined to have his Cambridge inaugural published because he was unable to verify a statement he had made concerning the text of a poem by Shelley A typescript copy of the lecture made for Laurence Housman was discovered and identified by John Carter late in 1967 and published by him and John Sparrow See A E Housman, *The Confines of Criticism* Cambridge University Press, 1969 For a slightly more correct version of the text, see A E Housman *Collected Poems and Selected Prose* ed Christopher Ricks London Penguin Books, 1988 pp 296-313 with note on p 506

48 Housman regularly used a medial for a terminal sigma see *PLWAEH* p 46 nn 1-2

49 Iuuen XV 7-8 'illic aeluros hic piscem fluminis illic | oppida tota canem uenerantur nemo Dianam" *aeluros* was conjectured by Johannes Brodaeus (1500-1563), and discovered in the Vatican manuscript Urb lat 661 (s XI inc) 'illicelu••s U (e in o mutato et supra scripto serpentes, ut corrector uoluisse uideatur *colubras*) (Housman) The 'best manuscript gives *illicaeruleos*, others *illic caeruleos* For Housman s use of the Vatican manuscript which was examined on his behalf by E O Winstedt and Georges Périnelle see *The Classical Papers of Gilbert Highet* ed R J Ball New York Columbia University Press, 1983, pp 291 sq

50 The author of the article was Friedrich Vollmer (1867-1923) For Vollmer see Hans Rubenbauer *Jahresbericht über die Fortschritte der klassischen Altertumswissenschaft* 202, 1925 (*Biographisches Jahrbuch* 44), pp 68-103

(45) Letter to Stephen Gaselee, a gourmet with whom Housman dined **Housman, aside from his interest in the classics and literature, took pleasure in food and wine When he could afford to do so, he began annual visits to the Continent, especially to France, to dine in fine restaurants and to examine ecclesiastical architecture Thus, in Paris, he regularly visited La Tour d'Argent where Fédéric created Barbue Housman" in his honor [51]

In 1930, Housman was completing the fifth and final volume of his edition of Manilius, albeit in 1932 he produced as well an editio minor of this astrological poet

Trinity College
Cambridge
4 Aug 1930

Dear Gaselee
    I am going away on Saturday and had intended to be absent about 3 weeks, so that I can be back on the 30th to swallow your fragrant bait
    I have abstained from getting the book you mention because it might conceivably, though not probably, delay me a bit in getting out my last book of Manilius If it sticks to Nonnus it cannot go much into the technical minutiae of astrology and therefore will not be formidable in that respect [52]

Yours sincerely

A F Housman

UCLA Special Collections Ms 100 box 72

(46) Letter to Arnold Rubin

Trinity College
Cambridge
England
1 March 1931

Dear Mr Rubin
    I am glad to have news of you and interested to hear that you have returned from North Carolina As you ask about my doings I may say that I have published the 5th and last volume of my chief work an edition of the Latin astrological poet Manilius I do not send you a copy as it would shock you very much it is so dull that few professed scholars can read it probably not one in the whole United States But I rank much higher among English scholars than among English poets

Yours faithfully

A E Housman

UCLA Special Collections Ms 100 box 45

(47) *Application to the Electors to the Corpus Professorship of Latin from Eduard Fraenkel, s l* (1934) **In 1926, Wilamowitz's student Fraenkel reviewed Housman's edition of Lucan in *Gnomon* It was a lengthy critique and led others in Germany to re-evaluate Housman s work and to conclude that he was the leading Latinist in Great Britain In 1934, Fraenkel like many of Jewish origin, found it necessary to leave Germany Temporary shelter was afforded him in Cambridge In this same year the Latin Chair in Oxford became vacant, and Fraenkel was a candidate with Housman as one of his sponsors "I cannot say sincerely that I wish Dr Fraenkel to obtain the Corpus Professorship as I would rather that he should be my successor in Cambridge " When a commentator complained at the appointment

51 For the recipe see Naiditch Miscellanea Housmanniana *Housman Society Journal* 21 1995, pp 8-10

52 Probably, Viktor Stegemann *Astrologie und Universalgeschichte Studien und Interpretationen zu den Dionysiaka des Nonnos von Panopolis*, Leipzig/Berlin 1930

of a foreigner, Fraenkel's supporters at Oxford summoned Housman to make a public response on Fraenkel's behalf, and his dismissal of the criticism ended that controversy

UCLA Special Collections collection 1551 box 21 no 823

ENGLISH PROSE

Case 5

In 1892 evaluating Housman's candidacy for the Latin Chair at University College London, W P Ker observed "That Mr Housman is more than a formal commentator is proved by the attractive style of his essays' [53] In the years that followed Housman was called upon to compose letters variously on behalf of the Fellows of Trinity College Cambridge, and on behalf of the University of Cambridge [54] They are models of their kind, their tone and meaning combining with their rhythm and diction to produce highly effective statements But it was his essays, in the prefaces to his editions and in his published lectures that especially excited admiration In 1931, Herbert Read and Bonamy Dobree included an extract from Housman's Manilius in their *Anthology of English Prose* The first anthology dedicated solely to Housman's prose appeared thirty years later

(48) A E Housman *Introductory Lecture delivered before the Faculties of Arts and Laws and of Science in University College, London, October 3, 1892*, Cambridge Printed at the University Press, 1933 **One of 100 copies "No 32, for Tom Balston from John Carter" This lecture, designed to reconcile the conflicting claims of the sciences and the humanities by affirming that all investigations are good, was highly applauded Indeed later in the year, as a fitting Christmas present for Housman it was suggested by the students that he be given "Opportunity for another good speech' [55]

It was characteristic of Housman that he fitted his talks to the audience Popular talks, such as his addresses to the University College Literary Society, were polished and witty But technical lectures to students were dry and competent—even so, ' when [R W Chambers] told an American classical teacher something of the careful tuition I had received from [Housman] in 1892-4   she said 'I feel as if I was sitting next to somebody who had touched God'" [56]

Private Collection

(49) A E Housman, "Cambridge Inaugural', *Times Literary Supplement* no 3454, May 9, 1968, p 475 **First printing

Private Collection

53 *AEH/UCL* p 11

54 Housman's chief formal letters are reprinted in A E Housman *Selected Prose* ed J Carter, Cambridge 1962 ed 2 pp 161-167 (= *The Name and Nature of Poetry and other Selected Prose* New York New Amsterdam, 1989) which also includes his 1892 lecture 'The Application of Thought to Textual Criticism   and *The Name and Nature of Poetry* For these lectures, together with the Cambridge inaugural and the talk on Swinburne see most conveniently A E Housman *Collected Poems and Selected Prose* ed C Ricks, London Penguin, 1988

55 *Privateer* 1 6, Dec 7, 1892, p 6

56 *ALH/UCL* p 123, where the teacher is identified as a Miss Deakers For Chambers's copy of *The Name and Nature of Poetry*, see below, no 53

(50) [A. E. Housman,] *Address to Sir James George Frazer LL D , D C L Litt D , on the Occasion of the Foundation, in his honour of the Frazer Lectureship in Social Anthropology in the Universities of Oxford, Cambridge, Glasgow, and Liverpool* [Printed at S Dominic's Press, Ditchling,] 1921

The friends and admirers who have united to found in your honour an annual lectureship in Social Anthropology, a science requiring no such link to connect it with your name, are not altogether content to set up their monument and withdraw in silence They feel and they hope that you will understand the wish to approach more nearly an author whose works have bound to him in familiarity and affection even those to whom he is not personally known, and to indulge, by this short address, an emotion warmer than mere intellectual gratitude

The Golden Bough compared by Virgil to the mistletoe but now revealing some affinity to the banyan has not only waxed a great tree but has spread to a spacious and hospitable forest whose king receives homage in many tongues from a multitude resorting thither for its fruit or timber or refreshing shade There they find learning mated with literature, labour disguised in ease, and a museum of dark and uncouth superstitions invested with the charm of a truly sympathetic magic [57]

UCLA URL GN 21 F86A22 From the library of C K Ogden

(51) *Nine Essays* by Arthur Platt With a Preface by A E Housman, Cambridge University Press 1927 **In 1894, the Greek Professor at University College, London resigned A committee was formed to select his successor, the report for which was composed by Housman The committee recommended the appointment of J Arthur Platt (1860-1925), the Council agreed, and Platt became Housman's colleague and admired friend (*Nine Essays* pp ix sq)

If his contemporaries rated him both comparatively and absolutely below his true position in the world of learning the loss was chiefly theirs but the blame was partly his He had much of the boy in his composition, and something even of the schoolboy His conversation in mixed company was apt to be flighty, and his writing though it was not so carried jauntiness of manner to some little excess Those who judge weight by heaviness were perplexed and deceived by a colloquial gaiety, much less unseemly indeed than the frolic sallies of Dawes, but striking more sharply on the sense because not draped like them in the Latin toga, and it was disturbing to meet with a scholar who carried his levity where others carry their gravity on the surface and was austere where he might without offence or detection have been frivolous in conducting the operations of his mind

Private Collection

(52) Letter to Arnold Rubin

Trinity College
Cambridge
England
17 Nov 1929

Dear Mr Rubin,

Assuming that you have to earn your living I advise you to follow chemistry or any other honest trade rather than literature which as Scott said may be a good walking-stick but is a bad crutch It cannot be depended on Maurice Hewlett when his novels were selling well threw up a post in the Civil Service intending to live by his pen the public ceased to read his novels and he died in poverty

---

57 For Housman and Frazer, see Robert Ackerman *Greek Roman and Byzantine Studies* 15 1974 pp 339-364 with *PLW/AFH* pp 165 sq)

And of all forms of literature poetry is the straightest way to starvation There is one living poet who boasts that he lives on the proceeds of his poetry but he is a bad one Moreover poetry is not a job to fill all one's time, and poets like Wordsworth and Byron who were always writing would have done better to write less

Others have asked me the same question, and I always give the same reply [58]

Yours sincerely

A E Housman

(53) A E Housman, *The Name and Nature of Poetry*, Cambridge University Press, 1933 **First edition **Housman's popularity began to decline in the first part of 1929 [59] With this lecture however, which F R Leavis and I A Richards of the Cambridge School of English regarded as an attack upon themselves (Housman reported them complaining that "it will take us more than twelve years to undo the harm I have done in an hour"), Housman came to be regarded by the new generation of poets as representative of the old-guard, and therefore to be denigrated [60] The old-guard meanwhile saw in this lecture an eloquent defence of lyrical, metrical, poetical verse "The Times summary was, we found, eagerly read and cherished by all sorts and conditions of people whom we had never suspected of an interest in such matters It was like a bugle-call, or the All-Clear signal after an air-raid the population stirred again, saying Thank Heaven that's over" For during at least ten years, the field of poetry and of poetical criticism has been invaded by swarms of people who haven't the least conception as to what poetry is "[61] Housman himself bitterly disliked this lecture

Following Housman's death in 1936, the modern critics he had affronted and the young poets, especially those who had abandoned metre, began regularly to dismiss him and his work The two went together Laurence, his brother, had published verse that was not up to Housman's high standard and had, in his memoir, damaged his reputation by various "revelations"

But the dismissal and contempt came chiefly from the critics the ordinary reader, conscious of the pleasure that *A Shropshire Lad* afforded, continued to read Housman

H U M O R

Case 6

Housman's humor is often wry and ruthless From his childhood Housman created amusing verse His family was accustomed to play a game, "Nouns and Questions", in which one was obliged to answer a question in verse whilst including some special if untoward, terms His comic verse, of which about

58 A similar letter survives to Mr Wilensky, June 6 1931 (Yale University Beinecke Library, Ms Vault Housman)

59 See Naiditch The First Edition of *A Shropshire Lad* in Bookshop and Auction Room' *Housman New Perspectives* edd A Holden/R Birch, London Macmillan (forthcoming)

60 H to L Housman, May 20, 1933 L Housman, *A E H* London 1937 p 185 = *Letters* p 335

61 J C Squire, *London Mercury* 28 June 1933, reprinted in Philip Gardner *A E Housman the Critical Heritage* London/New York Routledge 1992 pp 238 sq It is to be noted that T S Eliot admired the lecture where his followers did not

seventy pieces survive, often appears in anthologies, and has recently been partly collected in *Unkind to Unicorns* [62]

Housman's humor is not limited to his verse His formal prose compositions also are often enlivened with remarks designed to amuse the reader, usually however at the expense of another scholar For example, he concluded a review of W J Stone s *On the Use of Classical Metres in English* thus [63]

> The long and short of the matter is this We now regulate English verse by the strong and determinate element of stress its management is what distinguishes verse from prose The weak and indeterminate element of quantity we subordinate its management is one of the many things which distinguish not verse from prose but good verse from bad Mr Stone proposes that we should put the weak to the work of the strong, and subject the strong to the predominance of the weak Summer is come, and cricket is playing everywhere If Mr Stone will accost the next eleven he sees in the field and advise them to run after the ball on their hands and pick it up with their feet he will hear some very good criticism of his quantitative hexameters

And, often enough in the middle of the humorous statement, there will be an original observation that advances knowledge of the subject particularly in hand

(54) A E Housman, *A Morning with the Royal Family Illustrated by Frederick Childs* Los Angeles The Green Horn Press, 1941 **Printed by Mary Treanor and Robin Park in 125 copies This *jeu d esprit* was composed around Christmas 1879 and published, without the author's leave, in *The Bromsgrovian* of 1882 The Headmaster cancelled one chapter, on the state religion of the Kingdom and arranged for two offending words to be covered with slips carrying more innocuous terms [64] Many years later, Housman created a brief sequel, "An Afternoon with the Royal Family", not yet published [65]

(55) Mrs E W Symons, *Memories of A E Housman* Bath J Grant Melluish, 1936 **Pamphlet reprinted from *The Edwardian* including the [first] publication of her brother's pleasant verse —

> Amelia mixed some mustard
>   She mixed it strong and thick
> She put it in the custard
>   And made her mother sick
> And showing satisfaction
>   By many a loud huzza
> ' Observe " said she 'the action
>   Of mustard on mamma

---

62 The principal publications including Housman s light verse include *Ye Rounde Table*, Oxford 1878 (cf T Burns Haber *Journal of English and Germanic Philology* 61, 1962 pp 797 sqq) K L Symons (ed) *Alfred Edward Housman Recollections* New York 1937 L Housman *A E H* London 1937 F B Drew in [D A Randall] *A E Housman Exhibition April 1-30 1961* Bloomington Ind Lilly Library 1961 and John Pugh *Bromsgrove and the Housmans* Bromsgrove 1974 For Housman s humor see also N Marlow *A E Housman Scholar and Poet* London 1958 pp 171-179

63 *Classical Review* 13 1899 p 319 = *The Classical Papers of A E Housman* edd Diggle/Goodyear Cambridge 1972, p 488 etc

64 Housman to D A Slater Jan 12 1932 Adelman Collection Bryn Mawr College Cf J Carter and J Sparrow *A E Housman an Annotated Hand-list* London 1952 no 4 = W White *A E Housman a Bibliography* Godalming 1982 no 71

65 Manuscript New York Public Library, Berg Collection copy St John s College, Oxford Housman Cabinet II (Sparrow Collection)

(56) A E Housman, *The Parallelogram The Amphisbaena The Crocodile*, Los Angeles [Jake Zeitlin,] 1941 **These three poems, originally published in the *U C L Union Magazine*, were privately reissued by the Department of English of University College London and independently, by William White in this limited printing Although nominally limited to 250 copies, in fact only about 85 copies were produced by Grant Dahlstrom The poems are illustrated by a wood engraving by Paul Landacre

UCLA Special Collections PR 4809 H15p

(57) [A E Housman,] "Fragment of a Greek Tragedy ', *High School Chronicle*, Sydney (Australia) March 1917, pp 27-28 **In Housman's time students were expected to translate Greek and Latin texts into English and English into Latin and Greek Few were talented or capable in these exercises, and Housman parodied a student s translating "through a brick wall" in his Aeschylean "Fragment of a Greek Tragedy", which in its second version commences with the Chorus enquiring [66]

> O suitably attired in leather boots
> Head of a traveller, wherefore seeking whom
> Whence by what way how purposed art thou come
> To this well-nightingaled vicinity?
> My object in inquiring is to know
> But if you happen to be deaf and dumb
> And do not understand a word I say,
> Nod with your hand to signify as much

This parody, famous amongst those with a classical education, has been often reprinted For his own part, Housman rarely sought to compose poetry in Latin, albeit his Propertian dedication to M J Jackson in the first volume of the Manilius is highly regarded [67] In his Cambridge inaugural Housman discussed "composition" and, as was his custom, at once showed that it was commended for unsatisfactory reasons and that it deserved a measure of praise on another account entirely [68]

Private Collection

(58) Laurence Housman, *A E H*, London Jonathan Cape, 1937, pp 245-247 **At University College, Housman allowed himself to be persuaded to present lectures to the Literary Society These lectures have mostly perished in accordance with their author's desire a fragment of the paper on Matthew Arnold, was published in 1961, one complete talk, on Swinburne, was discovered in 1969 in typescript, and published

---

66 See Ralph Marcellino *Classical Journal* 48 Feb 1953 pp 171-178 188

67 Reprinted, with an English translation by Edmund Wilson, in A E Housman *Collected Poems and Selected Prose* ed C Ricks, London 1988, pp 253-255 It was I believe G P Goold who first remarked the Propertian rhythms

68 *Ibid* p 297 with correction of text "In the nineteenth century Greek and Latin verse was written in England and especially in Cambridge, better than it had been written anywhere in Europe since classical antiquity itself but meanwhile the most important additions of the nineteenth century to our knowledge of Greek and Latin metre were made not in England but in Germany That is what history has to say about the fabulous virtues of the exercise and indeed, quite apart from history it stands to reason that you are not likely to discover laws of metre by composing verses in which you occasionally break those laws because you have not yet discovered them But there was the less need for fable, because verse translation has other titles to honour which are not simply legendary", and these he identifies

From Housman's lecture on Erasmus Darwin was published, in the College paper, a "FRAGMENT OF A DIDACTIC POEM ON LATIN GRAMMAR"

See on the cliff fair Adjectiva stand
Roll the blue eye and wave the ivory hand,
Her amber locks refulgent emeralds deck
And orient sapphires wind her whiter neck
She marks afar the much-loved youth pursue
O'er verdant meads the bounding kangaroo

'Tis he! 'tis he! your wings ye zephyrs give!
Waft, waft me breezes to my Substantive!'
She speaks and headlong from the dizzy height
Prone to the plain precipitates her flight
Three nymphs attend her in the airy chase,
The nymphs of Number, Gender and of Case
The vine, the myrtle and the rose they twine,
To bind thy victim Concord to the thrine
The startled swain in momentary dread
As the fond fair descends upon his head
Shouts the high rocks his lusty outcry swell
And teach the obedient echoes how to yell
Barks the pleased hound, spectator of the sport
And hippopotami forget to snort
On dove-borne car descends the Cyprian queen
And hovering Cupids mit gate the scene
The enamoured pair confesss their mutual flame
In gender number, and in case the same,
Embowering roses screen their transports fond
And simpering Syntax waves her jewelled wand

So, up the steep side of the rugged hill,
Companions in adventure Jack and Jill
With looting nice and anxious effort hale
To the moist pump the necessary pail
The industrious pair their watery task divide
And woo the bashful Naiad side by side

The sturdier swain, for arduous labour planned,
The handle guiding in his practised hand,
With art hydraulic and propulsion stout
Evokes the crystal treasure from the spout,
The maid attentive to the useful flow,
Adjusts the apt receptacle below,
The gelid waves with bright reflections burn,
And mirrored beauty blushes in the urn
Now down the slope, their task accomplished, they
The liquid plunder of the pump confey,
And seek the level sward incautious pair!
Too soon alas too soon shall ye be there
The hero first the strong compulsion feels,
And finds his head supplanted by his heels,
In circles whirled he thunders to the plain
Vain all his efforts, all his language vain,
Vain his laced boots and vain his eyebrow dark,
And vain ah! vain, his vaccination mark
The inverted pail his flying form pursues
With humid tribute and sequacious dews
(So through affrighted skies, o'er nations pale
Behind the comet streams the comet's tail)
The prudent fair of equilibrium vain
Views as he falls the rotatory swain
Exhilaration heaves her bosom young,
Tilts the fine nose protrudes the vermeil tongue,
Bids from her throat the silvery laughter roll
And cachinnations strike the starry pole
Gnomes! her light foot your envious fingers trip
And freeze the titter on the ruby lip,
The massy earth with strong attraction draws,
And Venus yields to gravitation's laws
From rock to rock the charms of Beauty bump
And shrieks of anguish chill the conscious pump

(59) *Unkind to Unicorns Selected Comic Verse of A E Housman* edited by J Roy Birch With an Introduction by Norman Page Illustrations by David Harris [Cambridge] Silent Books [for] The Housman Society, 1995 **One of 150 numbered copies

Private Collection

Case 7

Attempts to set poetry to music do not inevitably give pleasure to poets. Wordsworth was distressed that a stanza of one of his poems had been omitted by Donkin. Gilbert Murray, speaking of Brahms's setting of a song by Goethe, concluded that musicians were devils.[69]

Housman, like many of his time, was uninterested in serious music.[70] Even so, when composers sought leave to set his verse, he freely gave permission for them to do so. He charged no fee, but generally requiring British composers not to reprint the words of his verse with their music. But he had no desire whatever to hear what they had composed. This desire was, however, at least once frustrated. Percy Withers records[71]

> I thought one evening in the library to quiet a reaction so tumultous following the gramophone records of Vaughan Williams setting of four of his lyrics that my wife who sat near him was momentarily expecting him to spring from his chair and rush headlong out of the room, and the torment was still on his suffused and angry visage when the records were finished, and I first realized the havoc my mistaken choice had caused. I thought to soothe him by playing some record of his own choosing. He looked rather lost when I asked him to name one but presently suggested the Fifth Symphony for the curious reason that he remembered to have heard it well spoken of. At the end he made a non-committal and quite colourless comment on the slow movement the others he ignored

(60) *Songs from A E Housman's A Shropshire Lad* London. Meridian KE 77031/2 Stereo, with Notes by John Michael East **This tape recording includes settings by Arthur Somervell George Butterworth, E J Moeran, Graham Peel, C W Orr, Armstrong Gibbs, Arnold Bax, John Ireland and Ivor Gurney, sung by Graham Trew. Of these composers, the earliest is Somervell (1863-1937), whose settings were published in 1904.

Private Collection

(61) George Butterworth, *Bredon Hill and other Songs from "A Shropshire Lad" (A E Housman)*, London. Augener Ltd, s a

Private Collection

---

69 For Wordsworth, see G V Cox, *Recollections of Oxford* London 1868 p 291. For Goethe, Sir Duncan Wilson *Gilbert Murray OM* Oxford 1987 p 167

70 See *PLW/AEH* pp 131 sq. Bryan N S Gooch/David S Thatcher *Musical Settings of Late Victorian and Modern British Literature*, New York, 1976. See also *op cit* p 209 (Dennis Davenport, *A E Housman and English Song* MA Thesis University of Birmingham 1974 Graham Trew *Housman Society Journal* 18, 1992, pp 51 63)

71 Withers *A Buried Life* London 1940, p 82. Probably the recording was of Vaughan Williams' *On Wenlock Edge* sung by Gervase Elwes (re issued Opal CD 9844) Housman had given Vaughan Williams special permission to print the verses on one program (*Letters* pp 106, 152) and later learnt that the composer had omitted two verses from "Is My Team Ploughing (*ibid* p 199) The composer was unrepentant, affirming that the poet should have been grateful for the suppression of the two lines (Richards p 221)

CPSIA information can be obtained at www.ICGtesting.com
Printed in the USA
BVOW03s1614270815

415407BV00011B/123/P

9 781293 808917